YOUR KNOWLEDGE HAS VALUE

Bibliographic information published by the German National Library:

The German National Library lists this publication in the National Bibliography; detailed bibliographic data are available on the Internet at http://dnb.dnb.de .

Imprint:

Copyright © 2015 GRIN Verlag, Open Publishing GmbH
Print and binding: Books on Demand GmbH, Norderstedt Germany
ISBN: 978-3-668-20894-0

This book at GRIN:

http://www.grin.com/en/e-book/321054/graph-theory-applications-in-network-security

Fernando Docemmilli, Jonathan Webb, Mikhail Bonin

Graph Theory Applications in Network Security

GRIN Publishing

GRIN - Your knowledge has value

Since its foundation in 1998, GRIN has specialized in publishing academic texts by students, college teachers and other academics as e-book and printed book. The website www.grin.com is an ideal platform for presenting term papers, final papers, scientific essays, dissertations and specialist books.

Visit us on the internet:

http://www.grin.com/

http://www.facebook.com/grincom

http://www.twitter.com/grin_com

Graph Theory Applications in Network Security

Jonathan Webb1, Fernando Docemmilli2, and Mikhail Bonin3

Theory Lab - Central Queensland University
Wayville SA 5034

bstract

raph theory has become a very critical component in many pplications in the computing field including networking and ecurity. Unfortunately, it is also amongst the most complex opics to understand and apply.

n this paper, we review some of the key applications of raph theory in network security. We first cover some lgorithmic aspects, then present network coding and its lation to routing.

INTRODUCTION

he rapid growth in Global mobile communication networks emands new solutions for existing problems. Such problems clude reduced bandwidth in mobile devices and the constant hange in their associated network topologies. This creates a eed for network algorithms with:

1. least possible communication traffic
2. High speed execution.

he two challenges can be overcome by application of graph eory in developing local algorithms (Algorithms that require w rounds of communication). In this paper we explore oplications of graph theory in cellular networks with an mphasis on the 'four-color' theorem and network coding and eir relevant applications in wireless mobile networks.

RELATED WORK

hung and Lu [1] studied the graph theory and it is relation to any practical implementations including security extensively. or example, they investigated power-law models and its relationship with network topologies. They also proved upper and lower bounds to many key computational problems. Ahmat's work [6] focused more on optimization issues related to graph theory and its security applications. He presented some key graph theory concepts used to represent different types of networks. Then he described how networks are modeled to investigate problems related to network protocols. Finally, he presented some of the tools used to generate graph for representing practical networks. This work is considered among the most comprehensive in addressing graph optimization complexity issues in networking and security. More recently, Shirinivas et al. [12] presented an overview of the applications of graph theory in heterogeneous fields to some extent but mainly focuses on the computer science applications that uses graph theoretical concepts.

Network topology discovery has also attracted significant amount of graph theory related research work from academia and industry. In his article [5], K. Ahmat discussed the past and current mechanisms for discovering the Layer-2 network topology from both theoretical and practical prospective. In addition to discovery techniques, he provided some detailed explanations to some of the well known open issues related to Ethernet topology discovery and their use cases. For example, one might want to model the Internet in order to reproduce its behavior in a laboratory.

Breitbart et al. described a pioneer work on Ethernet topology discovery which is critical in network security [2]. They presented novel algorithms for discovering physical topology in heterogeneous (i.e., multi-vendor) IP networks. Their algorithms rely on standard SNMP MIB information that is widely supported by modern IP network elements and require no modifications to the operating system software running on elements or hosts. They also implemented their algorithms in the context of a topology discovery tool that has been tested on Lucent's own research network. The algorithms designed in this paper work only when the MIB information are complete.

Gobjuka and Breitbart [3] addressed the same problem when the information from MIBs are incomplete. Namely, they investigated the problem of finding the layer-2 network topology of large, heterogeneous multisubnet Ethernet networks that may include uncooperative network nodes. They proved that finding a layer-2 network topology for a given incomplete input is an NP-hard problem, even for single subnet networks, and that deciding whether a given input defines a unique network topology is a co-NP-hard problem. They designed several heuristic algorithms to find network topology, evaluate their complexity and provide criteria for instances in which the input guarantees a unique network topology. They also have implemented one of their algorithms and conducted extensive experiments on Kent State University Computer Science network.

There are several researchers who explored graph theory and its practical aspects to Mobile Ad Hoc Networks MANET too. Saleh Ali K. Al Omari and Putra Sumari [4] presented an exhaustive survey about the Mobile Ad Hoc Network (MANET) and They made a comparison between the different papers, most of its conclusions pointed to a phenomenon, not a routing protocol can adapt to all environments, whether it is Table-Driven, On-Demand or a mixture of two kinds, are limited by the network characteristics. Oliveira et al. [13] proposed a solution for securing heterogeneous hierarchical WSNs with an arbitrary number of levels. Our solution relies exclusively on symmetric key schemes, is highly distributed, and takes into account node interaction patterns that are specific to clustered WSNs.

From privacy prospective, S. Sumathy and B.Upendra Kumar [7] proposed a key exchange and encryption mechanism that aims to use the MAC address as an additional parameter as the message specific key [to encrypt] and forward data among the nodes. In the model they proposed, the nodes are organized in spanning tree fashion, as they avoid forming cycles and exchange of key occurs only with authenticated neighbors in ad hoc networks, where nodes join or leave the network dynamically.

Donnet and Friedman [10] discussed past and current mechanisms for discovering the internet topology at various levels: the IP interface, the router, the AS, and the PoP leve In addition to discovery techniques, they provided insights int some of the well known properties of the internet topolog Maarten van Steen [8] focused on the commonly-use measures, namely, those concerning vertex connectivity small-world property, correlations in connectivity pattern, an centrality. Unless otherwise specified, the complex networ measures are of an undirected unweighted linguistic netwo N = (V, E) with n vertices and m edges as the model of particular language sub-system.

Breitbart et al. [11] described a method for minimizing netwo monitoring overhead based on Shortest Path Tree (SP1 protocol. They describe two different variations of th problem: the A-Problem and the E-Problem, and show th there is a significant difference between them. They als proved that finding optimal solutions is NP-hard for bot variations, and propose a theoretically best possible heurist for the A-Problem and three different heuristics for the E Problem.

Patrick P. C. Lee el al. [14] proposed a distributed secur multipath solution to route data across multiple paths so th intruders require much more resources to mount successf attacks. They include a distributed routing decision bandwidth-constraint adaptation, and lexicographic protectior and proved their convergence to the respective optima solutions. In his book [15], Remco van der Hofstad studie random graphs as models for real-world networks. H concluded that, these networks turn out to have rathe different properties than classical random graph models, fc example in the number of connections the elements in th network make. As a result, a wealth of new models wa invented so as to capture these properties.

3 GRAPH THEORY MODELS IN SECURITY

3.1 Graph theory

A graph is a simple geometric structure made up of vertice and lines. The lines may be directed arcs or undirecte edges, each linking a pair of vertices. Amongst other field graph theory as applied to mapping has proved to be useful i Planning Wireless communication networks.

3.2 The Four-Color Graph Theorem

The famous four-color theorem states that for any map, suc as that of the contiguous (touching) provinces of Franc below, one needs only up to four colors to color them suc that no two adjacent provinces of a common boundary hav the same color. With the aid of computers, mathematicians have been able to prove that this applies for all maps irrespective of the boarder or surface shape

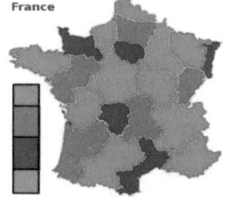

Fig 1 Provinces of France

Applying of the four color theorem in wireless a cell tower placement plan.

Consider the cell tower placement map shown above, where each cell tower broadcast channel is likened to a color, and channel–colors are limited to four, the task of finding where to economically position broadcast towers for maximum coverage is equitable to the four-color map problem.

The two challenges are:

1. Elimination of the no-coverage spots (marked red in the diagram above)
2. Allocation of a different channel in the spots where channel overlap occurs (marked in blue). In analogy, *colors* must be different, so that cell phone signals are *handed off* to a different channel.

Each cell region therefore uses one control tower with a specific channel and the region or control tower adjacent to it will use another tower and another channel. It is not hard to see how by using 4 channels, a node coloring algorithm can be used to efficiently plan towers and channels in a mobile network, a very popular method in use by mobile service providers today

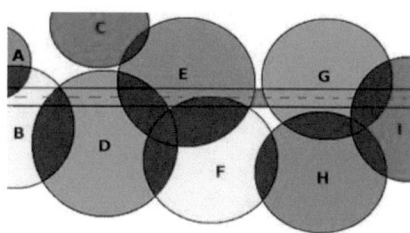

Fig2. Cellular Mobile tower placement map coloring

Node Coloring Theorem

As can be seen in the map below, borders wander making it a difficult problem to analyze a map. Instead of using a sophisticated map with many wandering boundaries, it becomes a simpler problem if we use node coloring. If two nodes are connected by a line, then they can't be the same color. Wireless Service providers employ node coloring to make an extremely complex network map much more manageable.

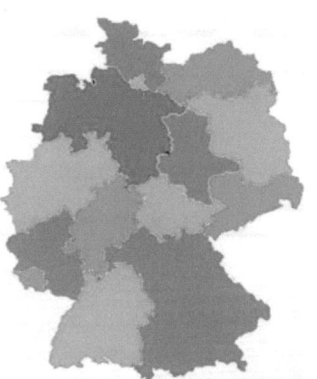
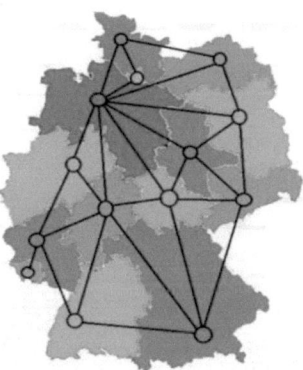

Fig3 A Map with complex wandering boundaries

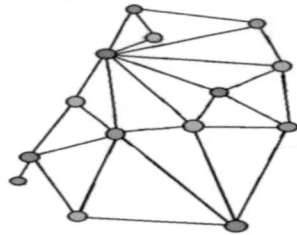

Fig3. The simplified network version of the map derived by

node coloring

4 NETWORK CODING

Network coding is another technique where graph theory finds application in mobile communication networks. In a traditional network, nodes can only replicate or forward incoming packets. Using network coding, however, nodes are able to algebraically combine received packets to create new packets

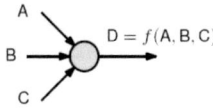

Fig4. Node replication of forward incoming packets

Network coding opens up new possibilities in the fields of networking. Such would include:

Wireless multi-hop networks:

- Wireless mesh networks
- Wireless sensor networks
- Mobile ad-hoc networks
- Cellular relay networks

Peer-to-peer file distribution

- Peer-to-peer streaming
- Distributed storage

Application of network coding in a content distribution scenario

For this application, the following assumptions are made:

1. The network is a multicast system where all destinations wish to receive similar information from the source.
2. That all Links have a unit capacity of a single packet per time slot
3. That the links be directed such that traffic can only flow in one direction.

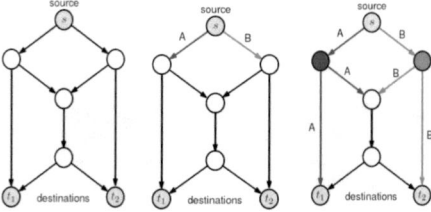

Fig5   Content distribution scenario

1st time slot

Following the first time slot:

Destination t1 will have received information traffic A whereas Destination t2 will have received both traffic A and traffic B as shown below.

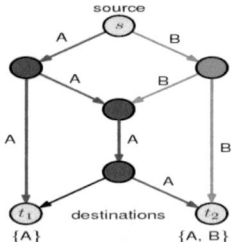

Fig6 First time slot

2nd time slot

In the second time slot:
Both Destination t1 and t2 will have received traffic A and traffic B and C as shown below

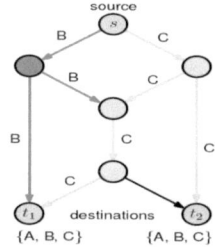

source

Fig 7 Second time slot

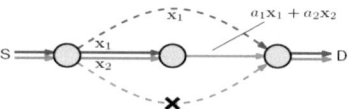

Fig 10 shows how network coding simply helps us determine how many packets should be sent by each node

Network coding application in a Physical Layer Network

Finally , when Destination t1 receives A and A(EX-OR)B, it will be able to compute B by B=A (EX-OR){ A(EX-OR)B}

Likewise, when Destination t2 receives B and A (EX-OR) B, it will be able to compute A by:
A= {A (EX-OR) B} (EX-OR) B as shown below

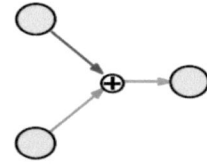

Fig 11

Network coding can be used with a physical layer network to enable networks benefit from interference rather than avoid it. Assuming the wireless channel performs network coding over the air. Fig 12 below shows how traditional network coding would perform, while Fig 13 shows physical layer network coding.

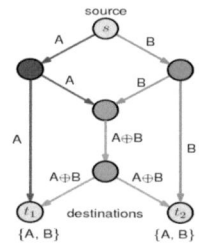

Fig 8 EX-OR Computation

Network Coding application in Opportunistic Routing

Opportunistic routing is a technique that makes use of multiple paths in a network to obtain diversity. Network coding can be applied in such a case (fig 9) to coordinate transmissions in order to avoid duplicate packets

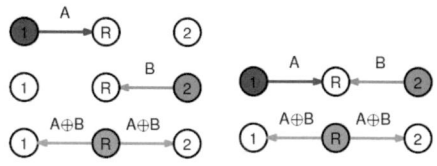

Fig 12 Traditional N   Fig 13 Fig 12 Physical layer NC

Here, the challenge is inferring w1 (EX-OR) w2 from the observed signal

$$y = h1x1 + h2x2 + z$$

Special case: h1 = h2 = 1

Physical-layer Network coding Scheme with BPSK Modulation

This one requires phase synchronization and power control.

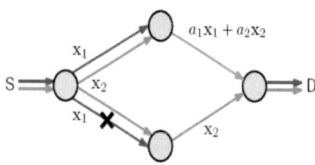

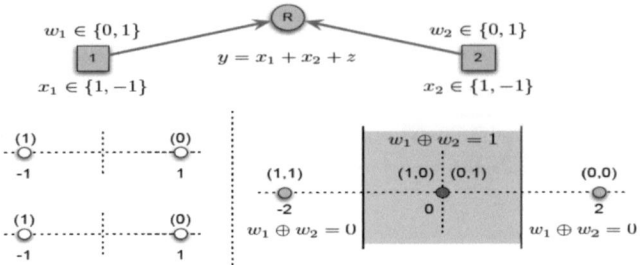

Fig 14 Physical layer network coding with BPSK Modulation

Physical-layer Network coding Scheme with QPSK Modulation

Special case: $h_1 \approx h_2$

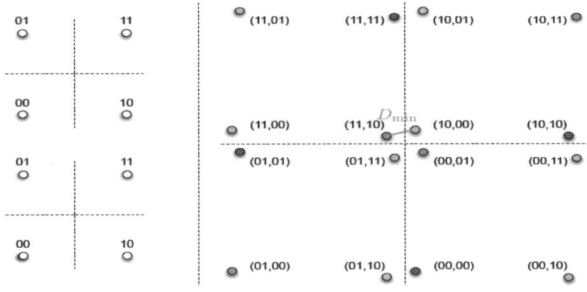

Fig 16 (a) Physical layer network coding with QPSK Modulation

Fig 16 (b) Physical layer network coding with QPSK Modulation

5   Conclusion

From the examples discussed it was shown that indeed graph theory, as far as the four-color theorem and network coding are concerned, can help provide significant throughput benefits for:

- wireless multi-hop networks

- content distribution scenarios

Other benefits are:

- Time, resource and energy savings

Simplified operation.

References

[1] F.R.K. Chung and L. Lu. Complex Graphs and Networks, volume 107 of CBMS Regional Conference Series in Mathematics. American Mathematical Society, 2006.

[2] Y. Breitbart, M. Garofalakis, C. Martin, R. Rastogi, S. Seshadri and A. Silberschatz. " Topology Discovery in Heterogeneous IP Networks" In Proceedings of IEEE INFOCOM, 2000.

[3] H. Gobjuka and Y. Breitbart. Ethernet topology discovery for networks with incomplete information. In IEEE/ACM Transactions in Networking, pages 18:1220–1233, 2010.

[4] Saleh Ali K. Al Omari and Putra Sumari, " An overview of Mobile Ad Hoc Networks for the existing protocols and applications", International Journal on applications of graph theory in wireless ad hoc networks and sensor networks, vol. 2, no. 1, March 2010.

[5] K. Ahmat, Ethernet Topology Discovery: A Survey," CoRR, vol. abs/0907.3095, 2009.

[6] K. Ahmat, Graph Theory and Optimization Problems for Very Large Networks. City University of New York, United States, 2009

[7] S. Sumathy et. al. ,"Secure key exchange and encryption mechanism for group communication in wireless ad hoc networks ", Journal on Applications of graph theory in wireless ad hoc networks and sensor networks, Vol 2,No 1,March 2010.

[8] van Steen M. Graph Theory and Complex Networks: An Introduction. Maarten van Steen; 2010.

[9] F.R.K. Chung and L. Lu. Complex Graphs and Networks, volume 107 of CBMS Regional Conference Series in Mathematics. American Mathematical Society, 2006.

[10] B. Donnet, T. Friedman, Internet topology discovery: A survey, Communications Surveys & Tutorials, IEEE 9 (2007) 56–69.

[11] Y. Breitbart, F. Dragan, and H. Gobjuka, "Effective network monitoring," in International Conference on Computer Communications and Networks (ICCCN), 2004.

[12] S. G. Shirinivas, S. Vetrivel, and N. M. Elango, "Applications of graph theory in computer science—an overview," International Journal of Engineering Science and Technology, vol. 2, no. 9, pp. 4610–4621, 2010.

[13] Oliveira, L.B., Wong, H.C., Dahab, R., Loureiro, A.A.F.: On the design of secure protocols for hierarchical sensor networks. International Journal of Security and Networks (IJSN) 2(3/4) (2007) 216–227 Special Issue on ryptography in Networks.

[14] P. C. Lee, V. Misra, and D. Rubenstein. Distributed algorithms for secure multipath routing in attack-resistant networks. IEEE/ACM Transactions on Networking, 15(6):1490–1501, Dec. 2007.

[15] R. van der Hofstad, Random Graphs and Complex Networks, 2011, (manuscript available at: www.win.tue.nl/rhofstad/NotesRGCN2011.pdf).

YOUR KNOWLEDGE HAS VALUE